Coming True

Poems by Karen McKinnon

*"Reality begins in the human
imagination, and must pass through
it again to be resurrected alive."*

-- Alicia Ostriker

Cover Design by Carolyn Kinsman

Cover art, "Mountain Woman," acrylic and collage, copyright © 1995 by Maryhelen Snyder

Photographs of Karen McKinnon and of the cover art are by Lynne Lawlor.

Book Production by Jeanne Shannon

Printed by Downtown Printing, Albuquerque, New Mexico

ISBN 0-9668073-1-6
Library of Congress Catalog Card No. 00-107474

Watermelon Mountain Press
Albuquerque, New Mexico

Acknowledgements

Some of these poems were originally published in slightly different versions in *Café Solo, Blackberry, The New Mexico Independent, Best Friends, La Confluencia, Wildflower* poetry leaflets, *New Mexico Quarterly, EarthSpirit Journal, New Mexico Magazine, Blue Mesa Review, Century, The Rio Grande Writer's Quarterly, SOL Newsletter,* and the chapbooks *Stereoscopic* (Solo Press, 1975) and *Spiralings: A Journal into Poems* (San Marcos Press, 1980).

Other poems in this collection were published in anthologies published in New Mexico: *The Indian Rio Grande,* edited by Stan Noyes and Gene Frumkin, San Marcos Press, Albuquerque, and *Queen Anne's Lace,* edited by Jeanne Shannon, The Wildflower Press, Albuquerque.

With Gratitude

To my husband, Richard Stibolt, and to poet friends David Jadunath, Harvena Richter, Jeanne Shannon, and Maryhelen Snyder for helping to make these poems come true.

Contents

III. The Man on My Pennies

IV. Stereoscopics

V. Cloudcrofts

Introduction

Poets are born, not made -- as the saying goes -- and it's finally a sense I can find no argument with at all. Who would do it otherwise, for what privilege or reward? And what even is a poet, or a poem, for that matter, in the chaos of our usual lives? Who needs it, and who cares?

Karen McKinnon is the consummate poet of any world common to any one of us. It's as if she took on the burden of thinking about it, the days passing, the nights with their various confusion, the places one lives and has lived, our physical lives on real ground and in a real time. The title she gives this impressive work, *Coming True*, is not finally the sense of a future, or of something only having passed. It's here and now that she's engaged with her life, bringing all to that consciousness and recognition. As her elder, Denise Levertov, wrote, "If we're going to be here, let's be here now. . . ." And likewise the innumerable bits and pieces, the myriad bags and boxes we've endlessly packed and unpacked, the securing loves and painful despairs, all the intimate *things* of our lives we've had by their very fact to bring with us.

It happens we have known one another
for a long time, since the fledgling days for both
of us at the University of New Mexico in the '60s.
I know that the world she writes of -- that which
is *coming true* in her mind and feelings -- is the
one I most value. It's the irreducible place of
human relationships, a mother gone beyond
reach, the "we" of a beloved family which holds
one safe despite, all the play between oneself
and that breathing, sounding, responding
presence of another, of the others one lives a
life with. Then, painfully and abruptly, it
becomes the isolation and test of oneself as even
the body seems to be lost as a refuge. "Coming
true" is not only a question of time but of a faith
which has only oneself as the possibility. There
is no one else who can do it for us.

No wonder that attention to the physical,
enduring facts of the world is so crucial. We
cannot live inside forever. So even a simple
movement may rescue the mind:

> Outside a birch tree quivers.
> The tips of its pointed leaves
> twirl suspended from their slender stems. . .

> ("Easter Weekend at the Denver
> Art Museum")

But hard beyond imagination when the mind itself becomes the condition to be surmounted. Then there can be no recognizing humor, no determining objectivity -- just the inexorable displacement of something gone very wrong:

> I have to make do with mere fear at facing yet
> another day enmeshed in hours without a center,
> doing time, the silent penance for the unspoken
> sentence of depression, a raucous clamor
> of silence without sense. . .

("Fault Lines")

If poetry "makes nothing happen," as W.H. Auden said, one must wonder about such expectations to begin with. Better to hold on to Charles Olson's useful sense, "Art is the only true twin life has. . ." Poetry is the manifest of one's life, its fact and company -- "some of my time now given to nothingness," Allen Ginsberg writes in *Kaddish*. Echoing even in the phrase, "Coming True," is another one recalls from D.H. Lawrence's poignant insistence, "Look! We have come through!" It's also Pound's, "you who think to get through hell in a hurry. . .," Robert Duncan's, "Sometimes I am permitted to return to a meadow. . ." and H.D.'s "I go where I love and am loved. . . ." We speak words, we hear them. It is the art of the poet to bear such witness, to tell as W.C. Williams "what subsequently I heard and what saw. . ." That is what poetry "makes happen," a sense of another person, of the presence of someone's telling, thinking, feeling in the world, as we do -- who is here too, now and forever, in these pages.

~~Robert Creeley

I. Objects May Shift During Flight

Measures Of Distance

Poetry is the passionate pursuit of the real.

~ Czelaw Milosz

Say we want to keep alive
what never lets go—the undertow
in the ramble and toss of thought,
the reach, the restraint of waves,
the sift of possibility
Or find a way to talk about loss
To make amends for everything forgotten

We could invest in the alphabet
Venture into tangents of language
(the ambiance of green, the taste
of grief, the feel of need)

We might hound the authenticities
of metaphor—those acts of identification
that hum for longer than the sum
of their parts—for which we are even
willing to rhyme in the hope
that the theoretical
can be made credible
We track the alphabetical
Hold syllables hostage
Ask for ransom and

race to net the true
fit, find the percipience
of wit, serve the living
nerve of words

Gathered

Just ahead of me
someone is walking
someone who thinks
the step
before I take it
someone
who sees the thought
coming before I arrive
at the peeling porch
and the new front door.
I can already feel
the sun-warmed brass
of the latch
before it greets my hand.

Is this the one who stays
awake in a dream?
Shows us the substance
of things unseen   hopes
we take this evidence to heart.

All the hip-deep winter way
home the sun glanced off
the walls of my head
and gathered into a ball
flakes of design patterned
to be infinite, in the way

a white knuckle of ice
grips the overhang
of the entrance.

My right foot lifts
to the first step
I took so many steps ago
indivisible as fingerprints.

If ever I drop out of step
again, I could ask to fall
back in—the way the world
does—for a day   for all seven
days from the very beginning
when with one breath
the word was spoken.
One to one
we make things real
coming true in this
traffic of ourselves—
and the latch gives—
we can be everywhere
at once, have been here
all the time,   practicing.

Etude

every so often
the shelf-lives of days
(partly cloudy but clearing)
shoulder a willingness
a longing for

the far-fetched rumors
of borrowed time

a willingness to fetch far
for time's every clear and
cloudy rumor
a borrowing which often
shoulders every longing

the will of time
shouldered
at every
far clearing
is rumored to cloud
long lives
with borrowed
selves

Impromptu

for the New Year

Kind of blue, this soft-shoe
shuffle through the residue
of last year's clues
pursued
as we always do
toward a world-view
unbejeweled with illusion.

Revenues accrue
and postage is due.
Still there must be a few
loose avenues or two
we could move to unglue,
loosen the screws
skew the crew
rendezvous
and retool
anew.

Disturbances Off Shore

These winters, we rest
in Tortola, the Turtle Dove
of the West Indies. We missed
the entire War. No newspapers,
no TV. These mountains float
in a sapphire sea with lagoons
the hue of lapis lazuli.

We plug ourselves in
to the parrot-green and hot orange
of the power plant at the edge
of Roadtown's dump
and come up fuchsia.

Sharp spears of Spanish Saber
rear under the blooming poison of oleander.
Just beyond the tenacious lace of the surf
off Smuggler's Cove, recurring reefs sting
with fire-coral. Sharks circle off Belmont Point.
Pelicans are losing their eyesight
diving for life into abundant schools of fish.
Wandering goats eat the heads
of flowering hibiscus.

The other side of day breaks into shadow,
Venus is diminishing, her rise star-crossed,
her bright coin spent.
Loss accretes on the scarred moon.

Gangs of termites build their housing
of mud cones in the palm grove, where
coconuts drop on the head of a donkey
named *Happy*, tethered to graze among
Birds of Paradise and other fallen blossoms.

Fear is keeping watch
here; fear never sleeps.
It seeps out
through every deep net, through
the sea-walls of dreams,
the dark mares of night, the shifting
ruins of sugar mills perched
over the bays rotting bittersweet with cane,
voices rising in watersheds of grievance,
in the abandon of quicksand.

Over the mating grace of flamingoes,
saffron and peach sarongs of rainbow
shimmer. We are learning by heart
these alternating currents, drifting
with this island.

Dusk falls fast.

A Comet's Tale

The constellation you asked for
was "deep and easy."
We didn't know how we could best encircle
the multiplicities of marriage
into one figure eight
but we promised to share
all the issues—our wounds
and wondering—as one connective tissue.

From our attending to that wish, comes this gift
to live every winter in Tortola, an island named
for the turtle doves in the West Indies, who sleep
far from winter's discontents while we watch
the comet cross the equinox of spring.
Our heads craned backward,
dizzy with proximity,
our single focus on the blurred ball of cosmic ice
and ashes sweeping up stars in a beacon of solar-
tailed wind millions of miles long
says *The Island Sun.*

We spring forward
toward the spinning top of the Earth
while the Big Dipper, its cup running over,
pours itself
inside out.

Passports

The Three Kings at the Puerto Rico airport—
these giant mannequins in plastic are due
to arrive at the manger today—Epiphany,
the sixth of January. They'll never make it,
headed as they are for the runways
in their gold rick-rack crowns and bejeweled
polyester gowns. Behind them, Mary, Joseph
and the Baby huddle in miniature, cast in perish-
able glass and facing the opposite direction.
The kings with their lurid smiles and icy eyes
carry boxes of gold foil (frankincense and myrrh
being in short supply with India and Pakistan
at war with each other again).

Between the kings and the manger
is a cardboard crescent of village
in Pepto-Bismol pink, sea-foam green
and parrot yellow, Dickens' carolers
cross-dressed from Victorian to Caribbean.
Pots of wilted poinsettias
hang their heads from dehydration
and there's no help for a few once-live fir trees unable
to survive their terminal transplant,
in spite of the bright gold bows tied to their arms.

Whether we're from Bethlehem on our way
to Barbados, from the island of Manhattan and
the wailing of Wall Street
or Martinique or Guadalupe,
we're dressed in the traveling uniform
of Earthlings: back-packs, Nikes and T-shirts

littered with slogans while loud speakers spurt
in static Spanish and people check
their water-proof watches.
Children cry and flights to St. Baarts, Dominica
and Trinidad are delayed or canceled.

On the mounted-TV newscast, there's trouble
all over the globe. There's no escape for us
or the three kings; we live on the same
planet of 24-hour Headlines from satellites
of our own making.
Forgive us for we know what we do.
Any investigative reporters from other galaxies
must have long given up on us, concluding
that we need a couple more millennia of try-outs
for Peace on Earth before we've evolved enough to
interest them into coming back for another look.

These are the times we've been given
to work with, spend our accumulated karma,
and bring forth once again
the light of the Babylonians, who read the stars and
set off to find enlightenment with no
global positioning system, camcorders, or life
insurance to cover what they might find.

How can we help but muse on these garish Kings
while we wait at this international airport for
small planes to tiny archipelagos. Any Second
Coming has to be born in us first, or we'd never
recognize it. How can we be, at least,
humanitarian Aquarians?

What's the world for, if not to wonder?

Our plane, we think, is announced in a spatter of
English and Spanish in machine-gun mode.
We sling our shoulder bags,
weightier with books and toiletries
than the artificial gold bricks
the Three Kings carry.
In line, we look like soldiers, uniformly outfitted,
weighted down with our plunder, inching along
a strategic path, vigilant in holding our place.
No time for wonder until we're in the air.

We squeeze into the slim metal tube of the plane.
We've not merely arrived, but departed.
We look happier than the Kings, making our way
to our planet's southern climates on winter get-
aways to the West Indies, the footstep islands
of colonizers, now filled with the gold
of traveling tourists.

We're a new constellation, crammed into the sky,
jostling with all the other stars. We read, eat,
sleep, check our e-mail, make amends
for things done and undone. It's our solar
system that ignites us.

Maybe those three Kings haven't got it
backwards. Maybe we have to take flight first
to see the star they saw. We could take three
giant steps together, looking to learn how
to tend the light, how to name and claim love.

Disgrace

I am sitting in this straight-backed gold velour wing
chair, so old it's the color of butternut, belonged to
Uncle Tom, no, no, don't let my mind go to his
furniture factory in Memphis, *that* could take me all
the way to the Pyramids   how I climbed to the top for
what? an empty and plain stone sarcophagus.
Even our Egyptian friend who'd never been there
before just shrugged, said he'd never waste time doing
that again, oh Aymon, your paintings are now in the
Cairo museum, the finest of contemporary art,
how happy we are for you and thank you for chasing
that obnoxious camel driver away, using, I presume,
ancient Egyptian curses, no I am just going to keep
sitting here for a mere five minutes, being fully
present to my breathing, three, four, shut the door on
everything else but maybe I need some props, say a
candle flame to dance in three acts complete with
stars in costume, but my god, I haven't even *lit* it yet,
whoa, how about some incense, just the simple scent
of sandalwood—are you kidding?? *simple?*   We
didn't get to see the Taj Mahal because the tour
couldn't ensure our safety there, some uprising from
political factions, a new war at the Love Shrine.
Instead we were held hostage in the best hotel in
Delhi where we got food poisoning--our fault, we
forgot that sherbet has *water* in it, of all terrible
things--what? Oh yeah, just breathe, don't smell,
taste, hear, see, just wait to be placid, linger, loiter, it
makes sense that scent doesn't help.   I'm not even
supposed to be making nonsense, my mind is an

empty pool. . .and reflected there is this Loch Ness
monster, black fin skimming along without a care in
the world while I am trapped in this chair trying to let
my brain waves wash away when how easily they are
set in motion, the slightest one-eighth of a thought
wobbles. . . I wish I weren't *still* flunking Meditation, I
mean Remedial Non-Thinking 101,   I'm filled up
with Thinking, my head's a Found-Thought Junkyard.
I'm supposed to be in Deep Peace 401k by now, it's
hard even to *want* to be lame-brained, empty of
thought I THINK Lot's wife was right—oh for god's
sake steer clear of the Bible, all that traffic and Babel,
I'm the lost cause of Orpheus, Mythology seduces me I
can't resist it how am I supposed to stop reading the
novel that Living is making out of me, drop all the
characters Creation Itself has made in the image of
Its own Infinite Intelligence, yes, yes, I believe in
You—no, I have *experienced* You, but never ever
sitting in a chair trying to turn away from Your
expression in and through me, Okay?

I should get an A for this admission and furthermore,
how do I even know when I'm *not* thinking? I can't
believe that meditation is a scam, but on the other
hand, who would ever tell me besides myself? There's
no more meaning in now than forever, wow!--write
that down, just let my fingers curl around a pen and
give me a piece of paper--blank paper, the only blank
I'll ever have. . .   Now then, in the matter of
Appearance versus Reality, the former is off-set by the
intermittent winds of intention
                              and there's no end

The Fair at Paraquita Bay

A thousand-pound sow
nurses in shifts
her sibling rivalries of piglet
Ninety-six hues of hibiscus bloom
under the blue prize of sky
on a January afternoon
in the British Virgin Islands
Booths offer soups of bull-hoof
goat-head, conch stew and
callaloo, ragout, barbecue
Roosters in spiked
hairdos tango among
the mango rinds

Rasta-man on a donkey
springs his rusty coils
of dreadlocks
free from under a hat
that matches the three
colors of peppers he juggles
A single caged iguana
displays a spine of eye-teeth
unblinking

He's seen all this before

Polarity Therapy

Make a standing appointment to lie down
on the table each week. Pay in advance
or you will decide you don't have time
for a massage and shouldn't spend
the money on it anyway.

After every knot and wrinkle
is pressed and rolled out
smooth as a beach in the Virgin Islands,
you will feel you can forgive yourself
for everything you ever thought
was more important than this one hour.

Now you are a wave floating free.
Through the translucent shells of your ears
you can hear the soft lap of the sea, the sea
saying over and over, the mind thinking up
reasons the body has already seen.
In the heart beats
everything
you need.

Pas de Deux

We have a conjugation
frequented by absence
faithful in proportion
to the distances
between us

It thrives on intervals
a disposition we have
for the contrapuntal
silence between notes
the reach
to opposition

It's a deprivation
of the daily
circling
into intermittency
This makes us allies
skilled in annexation

There's no lack of gratitude
for what is tendered by occasion
We've seen fidelity itself
consumed by constancy

Flung as we are in the air
of pure indifference
we are free to choose
convergence
fluent in the means
we have to measure ourselves
on a continuum of parting

What might we find
if this divergence
merged into the absolute
coalescence of the unanimous?

If more of us were handed over easily
we'd have responsibilities to less
It seems we turn toward difference

Easter Weekend at the Denver Art Museum

In a room of contemporary mixed media
a life-size vinyl replica of a woman named Linda
sleeps forever young on a spotlit dais.
She came in person to the Opening and
had her picture taken right here by this sculpture
of her, the security guard volunteers. We peer
at the perfect wrinkles on the bottom of Linda's
plastic feet, the blue tracery of veins.
Each hair on her head was transplanted—
that's not a wig, the guard adds.

Outside a birch tree quivers.
The tips of its pointed leaves
twirl suspended from their slender stems—
a dancer delirious with spring
and the resurrection of the body.

The Politics of Solitude

*With appreciation to the Wurlitzer
Foundation, Taos, New Mexico, for a grant
to do nothing but write, just write, just
write. . .*

Conjure nonchalance

Stalk words on a walk
Embrace ambivalence
Say the air at four o'clock
is a ginger-snap
and sun is splashing cider shadows
in the ruts of the unpaved road.

Let the shadows exaggerate
themselves into tall tales
Let the mountain come to you
Frame it, frame the view
(Chamisa blooming into saffron stars:
the miraculous actual intricacies of weeds.)

Assume the silence—these very
towering babbles of silence
in order to hear that you are
at the right time in the perfect
place, and being of sound and two
minds, you can make covenants

with the days and break them. You
reserve the right to be inconsistent
and welcome intransigence.

Flirt with your thirst, for
the random ransack of happen-
stance; flutter in the margins
of rumor and shuffle through
the vernacular while syntax
is in remission

Ride the day's vita, be excessive,
wise and otherwise run counter
to the hours. Hold yourself hostage
until the ends of inertia meet.

From somewhere among the dislocations
of words, discern the biases of incoherence.
Doodle apologias while you sink into
every apprehension. Recall what perfect
mercy it takes to make peace with the
livelihood of what you asked for. . . .

Keep time with the barking of the dark.

This is a solitary confinement devised
by your own known and unknown strategies.
Therefore, be certain that you do feel like
an impostor and resolve to look into

the very bottom of travesty. Make it worthy
of you, mutually inclusive, and while you get
on with languor, be contagious with the mind's
company you keep.

Keep easily uneasy while you chat with
your ghosts; linger among them; listen
to your whispers and appreciate how
inventive you are at talking back to them,
stirring up distraction.

Squander this surfeit and wander
from one end of each horizon of hour,
moved by the lack of having to keep track—
           I wonder   what June is doing. . .

Write an acceptance speech and revise
it twice. Freedom will always infiltrate
and scare the daylights out of you and
every new moon, so muddle, wait and whittle.

Feel as scurrilous as needed while you muster
the troops of your pledges and concede defeat.
Your synopses of circumstance are as authentic,
intrepid, and steadfast as you can make them.
You have become as enduring as it takes, you are
at last your own disciple,
spellbound by the platitudes of reverie.
Stop seeking similes for redemption.

Recognize the splendor of being
the edge's apprentice, the permutations
of aimlessness, and propitiate that faith.

Who ever knew exactly what
to do with vigilance?
No blame. Forgive yourself.

When you find yourself catching up,
catching on to whatever is enough—
love it.

II. A Place at the Table

Moving My Mother

She used to say, "There's no rest
for the living," and she was right.
She left me in the dwelling of her age
with a labor like Psyche's, sifting
through the residue of shelf on shelf
of every jar she ever washed and dried
and kept to feed me with her canned preserves,
her saved seeds of marigold, wisteria, hollyhock.

I thought it was done, this
sorting, wrapping, packing dispensation
of my mother's house,
these boxes of buttons, hooks and pins for
holding scraps of goods together,
keys to lost luggage, deeds and warranties,
promissory notes of things to fix and clean,
lists of stacks in storage, all the saved
folded sacks and bags
stashed in plastic
waiting for the future.

I can't bring her back from the underworld
where she lives with the demon of dementia.
She's a kept woman now, her mind the missing
pieces of lost luggage, her heart preserved
to beat on and on, as
day after day in the Alzheimer's wing

she is washed, dressed, fed
and turned to no purpose under the sun.

Night after night I dream and dream of sorting
through enough stuff to find a container
big enough to fit the savings of the life
she left in my possession.

I try one lid after another.
I wish I could cover, fold,
close it up for good.

Last night she reached out through my dream,
scattered seeds all over me.

Convergences

I draw up the indigo silk comforter

Your sleeping witness wakes
to my pleasure
in caring for you

Outdoors, an icy rattle

Crystal sleet
patterns in sharp spears
etching spirals
on the blueprint spread
of this bed

turning the earth of my heart
into a blizzard of grace

We age
age

Our edges blur

We want
less and less

besides this stretch
the longitude of years

Kevin's Orchid

I pull wild purple mountain iris and yellow freesias—
sprinkled with white baby's breath—from buckets of
water at the florist shop
to decorate the apartment
my daughter shares with you. She's waitressing
at the Marriott in Woodland Hills tonight
while you've cleaned carpets all day in Malibu.

Tomorrow is Mother's Day.
The flower shop's open until midnight
when my daughter gets off work.
This trip to see her—and you—
is a present to myself.

Browsing through the shop, I glance at your back.
You're on your knees in sweatpants,
gazing into the intricacy
of a white orchid blossom,
its arched stem curving over a low table.
You're much too tall to see it otherwise.
And you've got your tattooed arms crossed
behind your back.
I hope it's because you sense how easily
the petals bruise. They need a light touch,
a gaze, with the space
you're leaving between you and the bloom.

"How much is that white orchid plant over there?"
I ask the clerk. It's a bargain for Mother's Day.
I buy it and carry it over, to stand behind you,
still on your knees.

I feel as much awe
for your blossoming regard of it
as I do for the orchid itself.
Will a young man who draws
intricate pen-and-ink designs
like intertwining vines
honor the intricacy of my daughter?

Underneath her street-smart battering-ram
of an Aries volcano
beats a heart often bruised.
You told me over scallops and scampi
that you're a Certified Heartsaver,
a Cardiac Resuscitation medic.
No wonder she chose you this time,
someone younger than she without imperatives.
She's supported herself since she was fifteen,
dropped out of school to hitchhike with truckers
"so I can see the World" her farewell note read. And
because she hated the regulation
and rules of school. Schooled in civil liberties
by her Constitutional Law father, she chose
the pursuit of liberty.
"The World" turned out to be a place embracing it
all—the inter-galactic traffic of L.A.

You who've lived in this City of Angels
your entire twenty-seven years, the place
she chose to wander in—will you dive into the sea
as my daughter says *she* will
when the Big Quake comes, go overboard
into the ocean with her beloved Los Angeles,
an enormous flock of angels disguised as hellions?

You zip in and out of entrances and exits,
tap-dance with your hands on the steering wheel,
the dashboard, to the tempo of traffic,
a perfect pulse for this city of pulsing motion.
Bumper to bumper at 70, I don't have
the courage to look at the cars.
I watch flashes of red roses, hot pink
bougainvillea, bright white and yellow gazania,
their green leaves climbing
up and down the freeway walls.
I put my life in your hands, glad to be
the one who keeps watch on flowers.

I wish I could understand the street-slang
of the static Rap on your radio.
My daughter tells me Rap is "spoken poetry—
with the bass beat in rhymed meter.
It's sexy, *mad*," she adds.

Her rock songs are easier for me to roll with
than the beat, the heat,
of Rap's *intentional* sound—
another definition of music.
Maybe I could learn to like it
as I'm learning to like you.

Lucky for you you're a penniless artist
who can't try to ply her with jewels and clothes.
"I don't *need* any clothes," she reminds me.
"I've got my waitress uniforms.
Mom, you *know* I hate to shop.

-32-

Let's drive to Pasadena, walk in
the Huntington Gardens, see the
Orchid Show."

She's never wished for a Lady-in-Waiting.
Her first sentence was "*ME* do it!" at age two
when I tried to dress her.
She'd get impatient with the buttons,
dance naked around the living room.
Turning somersaults in my womb,
she danced long before she could walk,
holding on to the bars of her playpen,
bopping to the beat of her dad's jazz,
Coltrane's record of "My Favorite Things."

"Let me buy you a recliner
so you can put your feet up,"
I said yesterday.
"No," she sang, waving her hand over
the cast-off chair from the Marriott,
upholstery faded from rose to gray,
the worn love-seat,
a round second-hand table for two.
Her boom-box is on the kitchen counter,
her papers filed for safe-keeping in the oven.

Hotel chefs keep her well-fed.
"I don't *want* any more furniture.
I need the room to dance!"
I suggested that since she's been paying
rent in L.A. for twenty years,
I could help her buy a townhouse.

When she learned from a realtor
about property tax and insurance, homeowners'
maintenance meetings, groundswork agreements,
mortgages, credit checks, all the paperwork
she'd have to sign,
she backed off in alarm,
her hard-won freedom in peril.
"I don't want to be *married to a house*," she cried.

When this prodigal daughter flies in
on Southwest
for short visits to Albuquerque
I keep on hand an old red coat,
too tight for me now
in the thickening of middle age.
She wears it for treks in snow on the back slope
of Sandia Crest
where I try to keep her in sight.
She's a scarlet tanager,
cruising the currents of highway
from the ponderosa pine down to the cottonwoods
of the Rio Grande Valley.

You don't know I'm standing behind you.
You don't know that I named my daughter Shauna
(with a 'u' as in Faulkner),
meaning "Shooting Star" in Shawnee
for her maternal Native American
three-times great-grandmother.
She changed her name to Barbara
at age ten, after Barbra Streisand,
unwittingly following her
father's Isle of Skye origins.

After she saw "Braveheart," heard bagpipes,
learned some Scottish I taught her—
'what bonnie een you're havin'
for 'what pretty eyes you have,'
Scotland is the only country she wants to visit.
Though she knows she could never
sit still long enough to cross the whole ocean.
She did write her father that if her brother failed
to have any sons, it wouldn't matter.
She'd carry on the name, even though
the McDonald clan beat the McKinnons long ago.
Their golden arches cover the earth.

You do know she likes to drive up
into the Angeles mountains on her days off
from catering to movie stars and rich people
who live in houses beautiful in Brentwood
and Pacific Palisades.
She sees all the furniture
she wants to there. So do you. You have
to lift it to clean these people's carpets.
In the California canyons, the two of you find
penstemon and poppies, tarragon and thyme.

I hope you give her room
to stay up all night studying astrology,
that ancient school of psychology
housed in the poetic metaphors
I taught her to care for.
She loves the circles of stars overhead
like the Stars who live here below.

I hope you know you can't put a tether on Barb.
So far, I like you, your exuberant
enthusiasm, your wonder, the artist who spirals
inside you, spinning gyroscopes of line.
Has my daughter found at last a match?
Her triple fire-signs leap from the glowing coals
of your Sun in Leo.

Did you know that orchids don't need any ground,
don't need dirt, don't grow in earth?
They feed on air and light. If you were to look up
'Orchid,' you'd see it comes from the same root as
'Genitals.' Go on-line and you'll find it in a search
under *flora*, Latin for flower.
You've got a wildflower on your hands.
She needs to be watered carefully, tendered, her
April birthright certified.

I'm still standing behind you.
I have not, cannot, say a word.
I have no rights in this matter,
neither your mother nor your girlfriend.
I reach over your shoulder,
pick up the orchid plant,
its one white blossom trembling
on a slender stalk of buds.
I place it in your astonished arms.

Given

for Megan

These leaves would be enough, given
that they are green, that grape leaves screen
June's heat off the kitchen,
that they will also feed us.
Only our minds can catch
faster than our hands can gather.

They're more than we need
or can receive, yet grapes still
conceive their seeds in the soft belly
of summer.

Consider how nothing was required
of the lilies, save to bloom.

The Other Side

We're crossing that bridge, the Montaño
we fought against for thirty years—it's over
the Rio Grande with low walls of tile
leaving us free for the golden sand
the dark brown of the river.

September sandbars bloom with geese
and the light spreads through
the bosque we thought could not
survive the wounding. Still
there, the lithe Russian olive, green
feathers of salt cedar, spring-seeded
Queen Anne's Lace, the gold stars of chamisa,
everything overlooking the battles.

There is peace even in the empty grave
of the ancient cottonwood; its corporeal ghost
now shelters us with light in the absence
of its shadow, a space that lets in more
of the mountains framing this new arc
as it joins the sundered pieces of our city
bridging us from the West Bank of the mesa
to the foothills and back from the Sandias
to the sunset's angel-fire roiling over
the still lava of old volcanoes.

We let ourselves merge
on the path we did not choose to take
the one built inch by inch with the weight
we thought we could not bear
now bearing us over and over
to both sides.

We step back,
witness this
handiwork
and say

It is good.

Under Standings

Was a time once in snow
deep cold of winter hands
warm to the task I built
houses tunnels roads of
snow fast to finish a whole
town before Spring
watered it all down.

Blocks then, of red
yellow green teetering
fragile walls I hardly
dared to breathe around
for fear of growing out.

Sticks and stones woven
toward shelter cross-hatched
careful to leave a space
for the fireplace.

Weeds knotted over aging
branches looped low enough
for a roof or roofs of blankets
tented over clotheslines
card-tables tree-trunk stairs
to rooms for wood and sky—
of all things subject to seasoning
wood and sky
being last—
have lasted the longest and
still hold shape over me.

Mary's Dream

She lies in the bliss of deliverance
hearing the ultra-sound of angels
telling her *It's a boy, and yes, he has*
everything he needs to live in this world.
Fear not! Every woman comes a virgin
to birthing her motherhood.

Joseph has gone to see about a room.
The baby sleeps surrounded by the warm
breath of sheep,
and the donkey who brought them
munches on manger hay. There seems to be
no need to be anywhere else on earth.

Overhead on the rough beams of the stable
hearts of palm nod shadows
within the rumors of breeze.
She can hear a seraphim of stars
singing the night music of the zodiac.
This is the time of Capricorn
when it is decreed that what is above
is brought forth below,
on earth as it is in heaven.

She ponders these things in her heart
and leans into a dream of peace
when the lions lie down with the lambs.
She wanders, floating through the ebb and flow
of tides parting the veils of sky, cresting the moon
from out of the body of Mother Earth.

The baby mews and bleats and she wakes
sore and afraid that she isn't ready
to be the guardian of this vision.

She lifts the baby out of his crib
and gives him all she has.
It is enough.

III. The Man on My Pennies

The Man on My Pennies

Memory: an act of recovery; to mend by recollection

The shiny new ones take away his sadness,
make him glitter false with sunbeams.
The dark copper heads
of Abraham Lincoln are true,
make him look like my mother--heavy eyebrows,
lines curved down into Kentucky hollows
of cheeks sunken with the weight
of Sinking Spring Farm where he was born,
buckets of water hoisted up stone steps
from an underground spring in a cave.

No wonder they were cousins.
Even at eight I knew
my mother would go down into a cave
where she could not reach up
high enough to climb out.
We never knew when her frightening beauty
would surface again
to scare us with its depths of disapproval.
From somewhere far beneath her lay a black hole;
she was marked down at birth
for its recurring abyss.

My father's bipolar skeleton
rattled around in *his* closet,
his bones that could not stand alone.
Either he was full of exuberant energy,
or he couldn't get up at all.

We three kids were not supposed to talk
about our parents.
The illness was unspeakable,
a willful sadness, they'd been taught—
all their own fault.

When they could talk, they fed us
on a diet of facts.
Lincoln's father was so poor
he had only one mule
to work the farm. Lincoln walked to school
with a hot potato to keep his hands warm
before he ate it cold for lunch.
Lincoln was so poor
he had to play with clay marbles.
Actually, he never could play
because he had to split oak logs
to make the zig-zags of rail fences.
We played with our set of notched Lincoln Logs,
hoping we wouldn't have to listen
to much more about lack,
though lack with my mother
seemed an obsession
that fed on scarcity.

Abe was so eager to get to school
that he'd slide down the pine-needle slopes
in his buckskin breeches.
But he shouldn't have done that
because he was so poor
he wore them out before he outgrew them.
I thought he probably slid down those slopes
just for fun.

But fun had long slid off Lincoln's face
by the time pennies of him were minted.
Most of the fun in my family
was spent before I was born.

Why did he and my mother
have such deep sad eyes,
such drooping mouths?
What haunted my mother?
Even when I, the noisy middle one
who couldn't sit still, had been good,
had been quiet, had not asked
for anything,
why would I make
my mother sigh?

Lincoln had the Civil War to worry about,
and trying to talk people
into freeing their slaves
so he could "save the Union."

In my house, *I* was the problem
"Old enough to know better,"
unlike my little brother
and, "Why can't you behave,
be quiet like your big sister?"
She'd take herself into silent hiding
when any kind of comfort
she tried on our mother proved useless.
She'd disappear to a place inside herself
she never came out of
until we both carried
our own children's hearts
in the silent tomb of our throats.
They were bigger than the unswallowable
stone of childhood
neither of us could push away.

In the 'L' volume of the *World Book*,
I found the words of Lincoln,
a treasure far more delicious
than the acrid taste of copper—
or even the Mars Bar
you could buy with ten of Lincoln's heads.
Of the people, by the people, for the people.
Words trotting on horseback.
Words that forgave, like
the *Emancipation Proclamation*.
Phrases like *four score and seven*
that gathered up whole years and people too,
better than rail fences ever could.

Once on a good day, my mother read us
a fable from Aesop,
which she told us was Abe's favorite.
His mother died when Lincoln was only nine,
so maybe he got to hear it only once too.
The Wolf and His Shadow it was called.

I took a deep breath
in case of scary stuff to come,
and drew up some words
from Lincoln's speeches I used as amulets,
to say to myself in case of need.
With malice toward none, with charity for all. . .
We shall nobly save, or meanly lose,
the last best hope of earth.
I called on Lincoln's
better angels of our nature. . .
He spoke like a poet,
like the Song of Solomon,
like the Book of Common Prayer
in Holy Communion.

My mother's voice, full of lamentation,
led us onto the plains at dusk
where the wolf was full of pride
at his long shadow.
He began to feel invincible.
Soon his shadow grew so big that he said,
"I shall be King of all the animals."

At that, the lion tracking him
swallowed the wolf in one mouthful.

Then what? What does the lion do
with a whole wolf inside him?
I knew what was supposed to be The Point.
This Point was to never get so full of yourself
that you think you are greater than anyone else.
Was Lincoln eaten away by the wolf inside him?
He never forgot the cage of slaves
chained together
he saw in New Orleans
when he worked on the riverboats.
He vowed someday he'd run for public office
and try to abolish slavery, but wrote in his diary
that not enough people
would vote for him. . . .

    . . .*whether any nation so conceived
can long endure.* . . .
We *had* endured; we even beat
the Japanese and the Germans.
*The world will little note nor long remember
what we say here.* . .when of course
the world still did.

But somehow, anything to do with
my mother's talking about Lincoln
was like going down
into a dark smothering cave.

I didn't know yet about inherited genes,
but I knew people had 'blood relatives'
and passed down looks and traits
in their families.
Could something I called despondency
breed inside my mother
so that sometimes she couldn't play the piano
or cook
or water-color landscapes
without her work dissolving in tears
and deep indecision?
Did Lincoln store despair in a well,
dammed from his birth
at Sinking Spring Farm by still waters
running deep enough to flow into his relations?

I knew how much he cared for the slaves
who took care of him when he was ill
with melancholy.
It was always between November and March.
He was a winter S.A.D.,
a man with Seasonal Affective Disorder
before there were any paparazzi to tell on him.
His greatest deeds and speeches took place
between spring and fall.

He wouldn't have gone to Ford's Theater
to see a play that night
in the second week of April
if he hadn't been feeling better with each day.

The week before he was assassinated,
he wrote down a dream he'd had.
He saw himself on a bier, lying in state.
I asked my mother once if she had any dreams.
She shuddered.
"I don't want to remember dreams.
They're so awful."
She told me my father had a dream so terrible
he would moan and groan and wake her up.
Something stole his skeleton, his bone-structure,
so that he was just a helpless bloody mass
on the floor that couldn't get up.
I remembered this dream
thirty-four years later
when my father lay bedridden for a year
before he died of bone-marrow leukemia.

I savored and memorized
more passages of Lincoln's words.
Like the dictionary, they gave and gave
and kept on giving.
Words were my talismans. I couldn't imagine
how I could live without the world
I had in books if something ever took it away.
If you couldn't read, how could you stay alive?

When I was nine, we placed curls of red
crepe-paper poppies
on the graves of veterans for Memorial Day.

I said *The Gettysburg Address* for all of us,
living and dead,
that we should not perish before our time,
before Lincoln's steeple clock on the mantel
at home stopped ticking,
its pendulum struck still, cut down
by an ugly clatter of a gong,
a pummeling sound of iron striking iron,
its face of Roman Numerals chipped,
one of the steeples gashed.

The clock had spidery letters
that spelled *Seth Thomas*
on ragged peeling paper
inside a little door that opened
so my mother could wind it with a key
once a week.
Whatever she had or didn't have,
like Lincoln,
she had one of his clocks.
I learned to tell time
by its awful, relentless, gong.
My mother had passed it on to me
and I, like some chromosomal automaton,
wound it once a week.

In the late 80's, a friend and I
were reading our memoirs.
I'd forgotten to stop the brass pendulum.
Suddenly the ten o'clock volley
obliterated our words.

The summons of the quick and the dead.
That clock had not sounded so dreadful
since I was a child. I'd thought the clock
itself was ill, with its fretful starts and stops.

I apologized for the interruption, adding
that I'd get rid of that clock,
except that it was Abraham Lincoln's,
a relative on my mother's side.

"Oh no," she cried. "No! Then *my* ancestor,
John Wilkes Booth, killed *yours!*. . .
That's why we're such good friends!"

The pendulum of Lincoln's clock
keeps perfectly flawed time,
a generosity of and for the people.

Fault Lines

Who would ever have thought
I ought to have studied brain chemistry
instead of English literature--
or taken cytogenetics along
with the violin? Not that any subject
matters now that I lie in bed
my head bereft as a dummy
on a catafalque of thought.

I'm in the isolation ward, the morgue
of brain-plague called Clinical Melancholy.
Such a tame name for an assassin
with murder on its mind, this thief of speech
this siege that lasts for weeks while it branches
in my brain and takes on more terrain
with each assault
holds me hostage
until I can't make a move to assume
a new identity, break away from this impostor
disguised as me under utterly false pretenses
while it reconnoiters in spirals of faulty genes
from before I was even born.

It waits, this enemy occupation,
this prodigal legacy
of a brain disease, colonizing my mind
from generations past in scrambled tangles of
knots, dangling molecules from my dead head,

the weighty arms of the unwitting
wooden puppet it turns me into
until I'm only a shadow hidden behind a shadow
of doubt's bruised gloom of proof.

Even the birdsongs at dawn sound malevolent.
Their streaks of insidious twitter have robbed me
of another three hours of sleep's deep vacancy--
however ill-gotten from Alpra(na)zolam.
Virginia Woolf heard birds speaking in Greek.
I have to make do with mere fear at facing yet
another day enmeshed in hours without a center,
doing time, the silent penance for the unspoken
sentence of depression, a raucous clamor
of silence without sense,
an abyss of knowing dread
while the blades of an electric fan
twist on their shaft,
forcing air back and forth across my face,
breathing for me

It's only because this disease
has temporarily deserted its post,
tempered with a treaty of peace, a truce
wagered with an arsenal of treatment
deployed with everything from
psychopharmacology and electro-
convulsive shock to evening primrose oil, lavender
tea and acupuncture,
that I have the words again to tell,
that I'm well enough to say

how language, held bound and gagged
without a trial
can squeeze past the vigilance
of this prison of chemistry
and I can write in spite
of blood samples that can be counted on
to add up to precise degrees of disease,
at least a tangible asset of evidence
for an invasion that leaves no visible wounds

though I still bear the scar-tissue,
clogging every decision
from whether to coat both pieces of toast
with grape jam or marmalade--when I still
can't taste either--to wondering
how many hours I might be given
to work on this poem,
in spite of the marks imprinted on the cells
of my karmic chart,
in the lair where the ghosts of brain-stain lurk.

Depression never gets to the point.
It feeds on lack, holding grievances
behind my back until it withdraws,
bored with success,
and roams off for a while to seek out other prey.
Once better again for however short
a spell, I can be a witness in reprisal,
I can expose this assailant
of the mind's decline, leave tracks
as a path for others who might lose their way,

stumble unequipped into this thicket,
limbs heavy as a log jam,
thoughts bent twigs in a heap
scattered as a random pile of Pick-Up Sticks,

I want repentance, redemption
for all of us who've lost
whole years in the daze of depression.
I want us to know that we are not in quarantine
for lack of perseverance,
attention, or for any failure of worthiness.

Clinical Melancholy hides behind the inscrutable.
Yet it turns out to be mutable.
It's enough on your part just to ask--write this
down: *ASK* and keep it on a sign
in your own writing,
taped where you can see it every day.
ASK that this tomb in your skull open
and let you live as you again.
Forget belief—a brain disease can't believe.
ASK of the Universe, the One mutually inclusive,
the One that is all the goddesses
you ever heard of, all the mothers you wished for,
every teacher you needed, all the angels, nurses—
in a word the One who lives *in* and *as*
and *through* you,
the One who can speak for you. This one comes
in ways you can't even think of—
but you have to *ASK*.

Then keep yourself alive. You already know
this takes more courage than you can believe.

One day the morning's racket of birds
will take up their perch in the blackened
bare tree of your life and they will sing
with infinite improvisation.
The barbed wire snarl
in your head can't keep you
tethered when the double helix
of DNA spirals, loosening
the raw knot of your heart.

I am upright. I walk to the window.
A chorus of orioles in the cottonwood tree.
A green haze of buds among the thorns
of the Russian Olive. I turn toward the bed
I couldn't get out of for days.
I punch the pillows straight with a strength
I can barely remember.

The earth has turned me over.
I *asked* for it.
I have come undone
to a place where the
ground surrounds me
holding up my weight
once again, set free
on the extravagant Earth.

Clinical Electric

November cold. My husband
wakes me in the early dark.
I would not get up for anything
less than the possibility
of life again. To be able
to taste and smell. Talk.
Read. Move, be moved. Care.

We walk into the hospital
through the Out-Patient door.
I sign a paper giving my doctor
permission to treat my brain,
shut down in Severe Depression
mode, with ECT, Electro-Convulsive
Therapy: 35-45 second shocks every
other day for three and a half weeks.

An IV needle of anesthesia
enters a vein on the top
of my hand. Enough voltage
to wake me up begins with
putting me to sleep.

I wake, we walk out by the same
door, and my husband drives us home.
I'm not supposed to feel
any different until the fourth
therapeutic charge.

I might smile then, the doctor
had said, or say something to her.
I don't, but my husband says
my eyes are more alert.

I was told that in order to get
my brain back, I'd have to lose
some short-term memory. My husband
says we went to see two movies:
Life is Beautiful and *Pleasantville.*
I don't recall anything about either.

Not until the sixth
press of ions to reorient
them from the pressure of
depress-ion, do I notice
color coming back, filling
in the lines of the sofa-throw
with forest green, bright white,
ruby red.

By the week before Thanksgiving
I have become the whole point
of myself again, though
more exhilarated to be me.

If this disease comes creeping back
to dim and delete me, I can just
sign up for more current
and get on-line again.

I'll never have to be dead
as long as I live.

The Only Disciple Named Mary

He came to my tent one night on the beach
at the Sea of Galilee.

He was young and not drunk.
And his eyes were kind.
I knew it was his first time.
He wanted an older woman.

I kept most of my veils on
so my wrinkles wouldn't revolt him.

But he touched me the way a young child
explores his mother's skin,
discovering as he goes
what feels good,
what she likes.

So I lit all three of my lamps with pure fresh oil
pressed from the Mount of Olives.

I took off all my veils.
Afterward, I could always
bring back the way he loved me
with the scent
of virgin olive oil.

I asked him to come back the next night
at no charge.
He said he was circuit riding
with a group of fishermen, talking about love.

He asked me to follow their camp.
He promised he'd teach me to read and write.
That did it.
I rolled up my tent, traded my rings
for some papyrus scrolls
and found a pigeon feather for a pen.

We rode his donkey over the hills of Judea
and he was as good as his word.

He taught me to write stories
like the ones he told,
spilling over with poetry.

Andrew wandered off, sailed up so far
he came upon the Celts, we heard.

Timothy crossed to Asia.
James wouldn't launder his own cloaks.
He dropped out.

Peter got bored herding sheep
and had his own ideas--
which later hardened into rocks.

But me and Matthew, Mark, Luke and John
stuck it out
until our words were perverted

into heads without bodies
into thoughts without hands.

IV. Stereoscopics

In Payment

You have my attention.
There is nothing more
of mine
I'd choose for you
persistently.

Needs and Means

Since you won't talk
to me I've found
another lover
close as words
found the temper
when the words
chill hard
out of a great
heat

Grass, Spoon, with Lemon

Still
with life
all over

Inkling

What doubt is no more
than reasonable
in the loose-leaf
fillers of the mind?
There
is no word unturned
where it goes
without saying
goes even further
said

Kyrie

There is a space
opaque we make
to clear despair
so clear
things grow
there

Dance

We already know
the sound
of one hand clapping
against the palm's
lined cause—it's
both
hands we don't
understand
how they strike together
pause
and come back
for applause

Monogamy

Better to marry one
with several selves
than many with only
one

For the Love Of

Over the heat
of your shoulders I
see the cat, her fur
electric   released she
sees you reach
to my thighs   my eyes
widen to her purred
pleasure in us
the sights
of her eyes
narrowed
in lust

Morning Raga

I had forgotten how
light overcomes long
before the sun
ever rises.
Knowing no more
we think
all such
bare beginnings
are finished
and she who is wise
the sun sacrifices.

Overseen

The honest falls
so far short
truth must be
its conscience

Perspective

Those trees appear far
because they are
five lines in the mind
sufficient to shade
the approach

Pornograph

How obscene
the green's
leisure
caught
eye-full
under the
early
snow

Requiem

Blind sight to see
how things are not
What eye can image
everything that is
and is not yet
What have we lost
so often we've
forgotten that
sufficient to
the day is the fall
of all we call evil

To William Carlos Williams
and e.e. cummings

You
with the names of poets
saw how things unlike
(a white chicken
beside a red wheelbarrow)
could be likened even
unto themselves
and what i want to know is
did you name yourselves first
to fit
or did your names fit you
last of all?

after e.e.

the spring (trees) bold
in spite of the cold
hold a tender of green
and oh   tenaciously cling

Two by Two

You and I
are separate
and equal
so much else
is certain
makes that
possible

Blues

It takes more than
your life-time to
learn to listen
to all your lives
listening over and
over learning to hear
the wish your life
feeds to flourish

The Apple of My Eye

All I need
is more sleep
'Twill be then
nearly
perfect
only
don't
forget
to leave
a small
worm
by which
to see
the rose
surrounding

V. Cloudcrofts

A Faculty of Energy

in September
all the zinnias
from lavender to red
are bursting into death
the pears in free-fall
split
into the ground
everything is going
to seed
out of dying

Taking Leave

After the summer
empties the season out
I find a new tone
for Fall is dropping
over the green and gold like an
old shroud browning the cosmos
petals   the morning glories edged
with Autumn shedding more and more
trim down to the last core
of trunk and stem.

It's time to put the summer's luster
away   fall into a new clock
as the day turns to quarter-tones.
It should be easy to leave
the puberty bloom of Spring
turn off the clamor of May
all the hues and cry of birds
(their eavesdroppings beguiling the time)
the long sun of June's lunacy
the wheat cheek of August.
Those audacities are pressing down
to the ground under the wax spell of Autumn.

How fallible September is
already a relic preserving
the rotted fruit of Cancer
yet all the fermentations of
Virgo will not leave a trace
under the bones of Winter.
Libra's scales will rise
ring bronze
around the worn chronology of green
and plot another course.

Under my feet the vernacular of leaves
that time will tell sounds
the day breaking.

Daylight Saves

Tonight we fall
back one hour
The loss of time
a gain for the dark
we knew in caves
when the firelight
quivered with the
sudden blood of
our fear and silence
beyond touch was
everywhere

Only the cold
could be counted on
for more than an hour

Now we'd sooner be
asleep for fear but
even dreams don't wake
to start the sun
reappearing

Prevailing Winds

There should be ways to say
how clouds in summer's cumulus curve
no longer blossom on the wedge
of watermelon mountain
how the succulence of August
has gone to seed the ridge off Sandia Peak
with dark nubs of juniper
How the day is eaten by autumn

Aspens take leave with their gold
Winds wither the air into thin
vines of mare's tail, threadbare
ghost-rugs running over the lip
of the ridge
beyond the hold of this one sky

Rumors of crickets
sing their dying
dissolution
of a season
once
replete

Wintering

On the cottonwood grove across the cut
alfalfa field a sickle moon snags
the forked arm of a tree
Silver limbs languish after the hothouse
riot of summer when color revolts in
shocking pink   bursts in a daze of yellow
out of the ambush of June

Now there is the rich crunch of stubble wheat
a mauve lace of weed in a sun of pale
lemon-cream   not the blazing surfeit of July
when this field is the Gaza Strip
where the sun always wins
choking the ditch dry

How democratic winter is   content
not to scramble and clamor
like summer crowding in   taking up
all the space

Winter edging out   leaving room
for the crocus   a blossom lost
in the overgrowth of summer
Winter giving way to the tight
red buds of tulip urgent to uncurl
as desert willow forces up
the banks of arroyos before

the incessant demands of summer
to water, cut, rake, weed, spray
through the long dog-days of August
the torpor of heat and bugs

This is the moon of deep waters stirring
the almanac says
of water beginning to wake
under the ice

It is the heart
of February
a month where love
lingers

Grade Six

I'm going to abandon math
before it leaves me
any farther behind.

If a train travels
x miles an hour
and b gets on at c
when the train increases
its speed to z,
such that e arrives
at the one
and only right
answer—

I can see enough
of the prairie
to wonder
if a lark could see
the whole field
on *either* side
of the tracks—

an exaltation of larks
could see so much
of earth and sky
that a train, lumbering
across the prairie—

checking back for proof—
would see that a flock of larks
can fly ahead
can arrive before
the train ever left.

A Winter's Wake

Song for the Solstice

Now is the turn to light, night letting go
its coldest hold on the folds of dark December.
The longest night stretches out the shadows
feeling along the lengthening of its way
toward the day of the prodigal sun's return.

Light gains from the wane of the dark
eyes of ice, the cold fires of star-flakes
sparked from the bristling fur of night.
Dark is turning inside out,
waxing in measures of moon.

Out of the mouth of night
warm breath spins the white web
of the planet's branching,
springs to wake
the year's new-found hours.

"Brisk Winds May Exist"

and today, in fact
do rifle the tin
trailer-tops—
or was that word
"Severe"

I'm severing
a sign
on the highway,
Tijeras Canyon's
funnel
of ice and curves,
a way to get to
Albuquerque or
L.A. along old 66
which winds
like the river Meander
in Greece, once
kingdom of the
Hittites, the
Ottoman Empire--
Route 66 between
the Manzano and
Sandia mountains,
called 'apple tree' and
'watermelon' by
the *Conquistadores*

and long before that
"Turtle Mountains"
in Tewa by people
seeing everything
as one.

Whale Songs off Tortola

No one knows how
they sing
or which parts
of their humpbacks
chorus through miles
of undertow.

Easier to imagine
why they sing;
rocking in the undulating cadence
of the ocean's
unceasing motion

we'd sing too.

Mid-Stream

We ski cross-country
up the north fork of the frozen Jemez River
our tracks parting the icy lace of March

I lean forward on my tired, used knees

Old snow traces wrinkled crevices
of red rock overhead   fissures widen
The sinuous river of sky unwinds

Further and further we bend, aging into
the thickening bed of the canyon

Sun shatters atoms on all six winds

Complicity

I'd forgotten
the hot phosphorescence
of fireflies, their
C-sharp blink; how we'd
try to catch—in that wildly
flickering dark—
those tiny winged stars,
all the exuberance
of another season dying
under July's glass bell,
yet all of my astounded
life left.